the SINGLE DAD'S
SURVIVAL GUIDE

for Re-Connecting with Kids &
Moving on with Life After Divorce

Quantity sales special discounts are available on quantity purchases by corporations, associations, and others. For details, contact the publisher at the address above.

Orders by U.S. trade bookstores and wholesalers.

Please contact BeyondPublishing.net First Beyond Publishing soft-cover edition April 2016 The Beyond Publishing Speakers Bureau can bring authors to your live event. For more information, or to book an event, contact the Beyond Publishing Speakers Bureau at speak@BeyondPublishing.net The Author can be reached directly at SingleDadsThrive.com

Manufactured and printed in the United States of America distributed globally by Beyond Publishing New York | Los Angeles | London | Sydney

10 9 8 7 6 5 4 3 2 1 ISBN 978-0-9961486-3-4

the SINGLE DAD'S SURVIVAL GUIDE

for Re-Connecting with Kids & Moving on with Life After Divorce

Are you a single dad? Have you recently or are you currently going through a divorce?

The only thing worse than divorce is death, and, many times, a divorce feels worse, especially when there are kids involved. This is a book of resources for the single dad. As a single dad of four sons, I wrote this book to help the single dad not only survive but thrive and re-connect with their kids and move on with life after divorce. Life is filled with problems; this book is filled with solutions.

I'm not a psychologist, nor a doctor, but I *am* a single dad, and I have stood where you stand now. I have been in your shoes and felt your pain. I've dealt with all of the feelings of loneliness, hopelessness, despair, pain, misery, blame, and guilt a divorce can throw at you, and I'm here to tell you that you can not only survive, but thrive and rebound successfully with the resources and tips I share in this book. I've heard the stories from many men, like yourself. Good men who were totally blindsided by divorce.

Men who ask; *What do you do when your ex-wife cleans out your checking and savings account? What do you do when you have to move because the court orders it? What do you do when there is not enough money to pay your bills? What do you do when you can't see your kids, or you have a vacation trip planned with them, and, at the last minute, someone decides for you that you can't take them?*

The purpose of this book is not to go into the statistics of how divorce negatively affects future generations. We'll assume the reader is aware of those statistics. There are tons of books and studies that showcase these awful statistics, but that is not my purpose here.

Instead, this book is a roadmap and a toolkit for your very survival. It is a blueprint to succeed as a single parent. I designed this book to give dads the practical and actionable solutions they can take action on to see improvement in their children's *lives this week!* There are a ton of resources on the market for women and a few good ones for men. I wanted to give men a simple, practical, and profound resource to help them get back on their feet again. This book is a work in progress. We'll be expanding it fully to a print book on Father's Day 2016, and

there will be many bonus resources, interviews, and extras at SingleDadsThrive.com. I am not a financial advisor, so, when I talk about personal examples and make suggestions on things you can do to create more cash and relieve stress, it is purely anecdotal. Please check with a qualified, licensed professional when making money and life decisions that affect you and your children.

ACKNOWLEDGMENTS

Happy 52nd Anniversary to my parents, Bruce and Donna Butler. You're a true example of selflessness and love! I know it wasn't always 'heavenly' for them—as they can both tell you, it has been a journey that was well worth it, as their lives and testimony have touched thousands and thousands of lives around the globe, and they've built something eternal and lasting. They've come a long way from that first blind date in
Tulsa in 1964, when some guy with a band called the Charlie Daniels Band was playing. They have a relationship many would love to have. Thank you, Mom and Dad, for your lives, for your story, and for being truly awesome parents!

Tom Newman Impact Productions, it was a pleasure sharing an office with you and your staff in the same building. Thanks for all you do to get God's Word out in the form of movies.

Jim Bridenstine, it is also been a pleasure to share an office with you and your campaign team. You make America safer and are a true patriot and defender of the Constitution. When I vote for you again is when you are running for President.

Ken, my big brother who taught me how to play baseball. I still can't beat you up, even if I tried.

Jeff Long, Billy Dalton, Tom Kole, Charles Jones, Ron Isam, Todd Rutherford, Doug and Ted Shropshire, and John Locher you've been awesome friends and great strength.

THANKFUL FOR MY MENTORS

I am thankful for the mentors I've had throughout my life. Without mentors, we are doomed to repeat the mistakes of the past and regress. You will hear me mention several mentors throughout this book. Some I mention by their actual name, other times, because of the sensitive nature of their work and the ugliness of divorce, their names have been changed.

Antonio, "I had just gone through a divorce and a major custody battle. I spent all of my money and my energy, and I was exhausted. The tips you shared with me gave me my confidence and my self-esteem back.Me and my son thank you for the practical advice in this book!"

THANK YOU!

Thank you for reading this book. If you sought out this book or someone shared this book with you, no doubt, you need quick solutions, answers, and practical tips on how to land on your feet and make life good again.

TABLE OF CONTENTS

HARRY CHAPIN
"CAT'S IN THE CRADLE"
LYRICS

My child arrived just the other day
He came to the world in the usual way
But there were planes to catch and bills to pay
He learned to walk while I was away
And he was talkin' 'fore I knew it, and as he grew
He'd say "I'm gonna be like you, Dad
You know I'm gonna be like you"

And the cat's in the cradle and the silver spoon
Little boy blue and the man on the moon
When you comin' home, Dad
I don't know when, but we'll get together then
You know we'll have a good time then

My son turned ten just the other day
He said, "Thanks for the ball,
Dad, come on let's play Can you teach me to throw",
I said "Not today
I got a lot to do", he said, "That's ok"
And he walked away but his smile never dimmed
And said, "I'm gonna be like him, yeah
You know I'm gonna be like him"

And the cat's in the cradle and the silver spoon
Little boy blue and the man on the moon
When you comin' home, Dad
I don't know when, but we'll get together then
You know we'll have a good time then

Well, he came from college just the other day
So much like a man I just had to say
"Son, I'm proud of you, can you sit for a while"
He shook his head and said with a smile
"What I'd really like, Dad, is to borrow the car keys
See you later, can I have them please"

And the cat's in the cradle and the silver spoon
Little boy blue and the man on the moon
When you comin' home son
I don't know when, but we'll get together then,
Dad You know we'll have a good time then

I've long since retired, my son's moved away
I called him up just the other day
I said, "I'd like to see you if you don't mind"
He said, "I'd love to, Dad, if I can find the time
You see my new job's a hassle and the kids have the flu

But it's sure nice talking to you,
Dad It's been sure nice talking to you"

And as I hung up the phone it occurred to me
He'd grown up just like me
My boy was just like me

And the cat's in the cradle and the silver spoon
Little boy blue and the man in the moon
When you comin' home son
I don't know when, but we'll get together then,
Dad We're gonna have a good time then

Part 1

CHAPTER 1
YOU ARE NOT ALONE

According to Bloomberg, there were 2.4 million divorces last year, leaving 1.2 million men single. Not only are you not alone, but there are single dads who have been through many of the same experiences that you have.

In 1985, there were only 300,000 single-father homes.
Today, there are 3 million, according to Pew Research.

As I write this book, my parents just celebrated 52 years of marriage. They are more in love now than ever, and I am grateful that I was blessed to grow up in an intact home. The sad fact, however, is that many of my Gen-X classmates (I'm 47 at the time of this writing), and many Millennials (in their twenties and early 30s) are finding themselves raising their kids alone or without the support of the significant other who carried and gave birth to their son and or daughter for nine months, all of which presents a real challenge and opportunity.

I grew up on the farm in Vinita, Oklahoma with my parents and my older brother, Ken. Growing up in the country was a dream come true. Living nine miles from town with a tree house, barn, 30 acres, two horses, a motorcycle, and a one-acre garden (maybe it was only 1/4 of an acre, but it felt like ten-acre garden to work), I felt like I was the protagonist of an adventure novel, like Tom Sawyer or Huck Finn. I had many amazing and memorable adventures with Ken and our neighbors, Dave and Tony.

We rode horses, bailed hay, fished and swam in our muddy old pond, camped out in our big tent, and constantly had friends over. Everyone wanted to come to our house, especially the kids from town.

Church and baseball where my life, especially in the summer. After chores in the garden each morning, we'd play baseball in our pasture, until it was time to get on our baseball uniforms and head to town for the game. I played on the older boys' team, so David and Tony's mom and my mom would take turns driving us into town for practice and games. One highlight of being the second baseman and my brother, Ken, playing catcher is that no one could steal second. We'd played so many hours and years on the farm, we'd get everyone out. We'd always tag you out on second base! When I was 13 and my brother was 15, we won the championship game with only eight players, instead of the traditional nine. For those of you who know baseball, that means we had an automatic out when the ninth 'ghost batter' came up to bat. This, coupled with the fact that our coach was only 17-years-old, no one thought we'd win. But win, we did. We won the game in overtime, and the celebration was bigger than any World Series! We drank Dr. Pepper and stayed up until dawn, reliving every play!

My 4 Amazing sons Michael, Matt, Josh & Jeremiah are 26, 24, 22 & 20 at the time of this book printing.

CHAPTER 2

HAVE WE FORGOTTEN
OUR DADS?

I went to the Dream Center at Angelus Temple in Los Angeles on Mother's Day. I've been following the amazing work of Matthew and Caroline Barnett for years, and I wanted to show my support and see what they have been up to. I've admired their work with the homeless and suffering in the Greater Los Angeles area, as well as their work with restoring human trafficking victims. Being Mother's Day, Caroline shared the message that day, and she made an interesting observation, "Mother's Day is the most-attended church service of the year, and Father's Day is typically the least-attended church service of the year. I think the reason for that is that on Mother's Day, most pastors go on and on about the wonderful virtues of moms, and, on Father's Day, the majority of pastors preach a sermon about how men need to shape up." Regrettably, I have to say, I had to agree with her. This has been my observation, too. What about you, Dad? Do you feel bashed by those from whom you'd expect support, love, understanding and affirmation?

> According to Bloomberg, there were 2.4 million divorces last year, leaving 1.2 million men single.

In the midst of the chaos and stress of divorce, many times, we realize that we have forgotten about the emotional wellbeingof our kids, but I'm concerned about the emotional, spiritual, and mental health of our dads. What have we done with "Honor thy Father and thy Mother"? How many men feel broken and kicked to the curb by society, by the courts, by an ex-wife, and even by their own kids? It is my goal, by the Grace of God, to help you, Dad, get your manhood back.

Throughout this book, I will help you get your mojo back, so you are finally able to look yourself in the mirror and say, *Hey, I didn't do everything right, but I did the best I could with the tools I had at the time. Now, I'm ready to move forward and do the best I can for my kids and for my family.* That's the kind of man that you are. The kind of man that makes a difference and the kind of man that earns the respect, admiration, and love of his children.

Right now, even if your kids hate you, curse you, and don't want to see you, the day will come when they will honor you and respect you, because you will have made the right decisions in the midst of this mess. Even though much of the mess or even all of the mess may be your fault. You can eventually come to the point at which you feel peace and they feel peace, because you have moved on into an emotionally healthy place, taken ownership of your life and your actions, and they see it, feel it, know it ,and are at peace with it. That is my goal for you: that not only will you be able to look yourself in the mirror and feel good and believe it when you tell yourself in that mirror, "You are a good dad!", but you can also be proud of the fact that, by God's Grace, you can hold your head up high, and your kids can be proud to call you "Dad".

In many states and in many situations the courts don't favor dads. It seems like, to many divorced dads that "the system" and the courts have been stacked against them. The thing to remember here is being in your children's life after the divorce won't be easy but long term stability can be the result of Fatherly patience and persistence on our part. It will take a prolonged, life-time of effort.

Like treading water on the open ocean so our kids can be supported by the sole life preserver in the boat, so a divorce is like a capsized boat and as men we will need help, courage and resources to be present for our children and guide them to safety, confidence and success as growing young adults with families of their own.

CHAPTER 3

I'M A PROUD DAD,
TIMES 4

My youngest son, Jeremiah, just graduated from high school with the honor of Top Culinary Student in Oklahoma. I'm so proud of him and my other three sons. Michael, Jr. is 25, Matt is 23, Josh is 21, and Jeremiah is 18. It seems like yesterday that they were ten, eight, six, and four and their mother and I were navigating the shark-infested waters of divorce court.

I've got to admit, even though I've come to have a good relationship with all four of my sons over the years, it wasn't always this way. There were times they were processing their own anger over our divorce, and they did not want to spend time with me. Many of you may be going through something similar right now, and it hurts, but you have to respect your kids during this time and give them some space. It's during these times that they are testing you, to see if you will still love them and be there for them when they tell you they hate you and don't want to see you again.

Let's try to look at life through their perspective for just a bit: their world just got turned upside-down. Everything about their security, their emotional health, and their peace got thrown out the window with mom and dad screaming in the background. Studies show that kids never let go of the dream that their parents will get back together someday—it is simply the way that they are wired. Unfortunately, divorce negatively affects our kids. It ages them, jades them, destroys trust, causes them to question everything, and can even rob them of their sense of security, identity, and motivation.

This is not a book about the trauma of divorce, the reasons for divorce or how much divorce hurts parents and kids.

This book is a survival guide for single dads who are going through a divorce, are recently divorced or find themselves single again after a relationship has ended. Regardless if you wanted the relationship to end or not, dad's, men, here we are and here we go. There is a light at the end of the tunnel at it is not a train!

So my goal with this book is to help you as a single man cope with the loss of a supportive relationship and to give you the tools not only just to survive but to thrive!

This is not a book for victims. This is not a book for wimps. I wrote this book to help you succeed and I really believe you now have the resources you need to rebound successfully and to minimize the trauma and loss in your life and in the life of your kids.

Research shows nothing is more traumatic in life than a divorce other than death.

The **Holmes and Rahe stress scale** is a list of 43 stressful life events that can contribute to illness. In 1967, psychiatrists Thomas Holmes and Richard Rahe examined the medical records of over 5,000 medical patients as a way to determine whether stressful events might cause illnesses. Patients were asked to tally a list of 43 life events based on a relative score. A positive correlation of 0.118 was found between their life events and their illnesses.

Holmes and Rahe Stress Scale

Life Event	Value	Life Event	Value
Death of Spouse	100	Trouble with In-Laws	29
Divorce	73	Spouse Begins or Stops Work	26
Marital Separation	65	Begin or End School	26
Jail Term	63	Change in Living Conditions	25
Death of Close Family Member	63	Revision of Personal Habits	24
Personal Injury or Illness	53	Trouble with Boss	23
Marriage	50	Change in Work Hours	20
Fired at Work	47	Change in Residence	20
Marital Reconciliation	45	Change in Schools	20
Retirement	45	Change in Recreation	19
Change in Health of Family	44	Change in Church Activities	19
Pregnancy	40	Change in Social Activities	18
Sex Difficulties	39	Change in Sleeping Habits	16
Gain New Family Member	39	Change in Eating Habits	15
Business Readjustment	39	Vacation	13
Change in Financial State	38	Christmas	12
Death of a Close Friend	37	Minor Violations of the Law	11

Their results were published as the Social Readjustment Rating Scale (SRRS), known more commonly as the Holmes and Rahe Stress Scale. Subsequent validation has supported the links between stress and illness.

Score of 300+:   At risk of illness.

Score of 150-299:   Risk of illness is moderate (reduced by 30%from the above risk).

Score <150:   Only have a slight risk of illness.

Take a look at this scale and see how many life impacting events you have been through and how this can affect your emotional, mental and spiritual state now.

They conducted a similar study on children and I include the results of their findings with a similar visual graph in **Chapter 9 How to Raise Emotionally Healthy Children.**

Many commentators have said for years that divorce is worse than death because many times with death there is closure but with a divorce closure, especially when kids are involved can be hard to find.

In the last chapter of this book I give a complete list of resources and tools to help you as the single dad and your kids thrive with money, kids, relationships, emotional health and spiritual health

The situation you find yourself in today, facing divorce, is more real than a reality TV show and the clock is counting down. Your very survival and the survival of your children is on a race against the clock and against your ability to emotionally, mentally, financially and spiritually re-connect with your life purpose and navigate your family to safer waters. What you do now can have an historic impact on your families future financially, emotionally, spiritually and socially.

If your divorce finds you requiring a career change and or geography change your stress factors multiply many times over.

This is like you being chosen for the toughest season of survivor with all of the world watching, except there are no green rooms, rehearsals, do-over's, phone a friend, or lifeline's available. The only thing in your backpack is a calculator, 1 book of your choice, a knife, 1 match, a flashlight and an empty water bottle.

So buckle up and let's go for the ride of your life!

Definition of SURVIVAL

Sur•viv•al

the state or fact of continuing to live or exist, typically in spite of an accident, ordeal, or difficult circumstances.

"the animal's chances of survival were pretty low"

In this book, I don't dwell on the past. This is not a "How To" book on how to fix your marriage. This is a book about your financial, emotional, physical and spiritual survival once you marriage has ended or is in the process of ending.

As someone who's been through a life altering divorce more than once I've been there. I've experienced not just the pain and trauma of divorce but also the guilt, stigma, pains, awkwardness, economic upheaval and all of the other things that come with it.

This is not a book about the trauma of divorce, the reasons for divorce or how much divorce hurts parents and kids. This is a book for survivors, for warriors for leaders. For the men that have lost their marriages and their kids but refuse to give up, roll over or play dead. It's about getting yourself, your brain and your cajones back in the game of life and moving forward, after all this is what's best for you and your kids right?

Part 2

CHAPTER 1

YOU WANT A WHAT?

"When you are single, all you see is happy married people; when you are married, all you see is happy single people."

Michael D. Butler

The Re-Occurring Nightmare

I awoke in a panic, breaking out in a cold sweat and gasping for air. I'd had this dream—rather, this nightmare—countless times before, but, this time, it seemed more real than ever. I was only 5 years old, and it was in the middle of the night. I turned on the bedroom light to make sure my seven-year-old brother was still on the top bunk bed in our small, three-bedroom home in rural Oklahoma. Calming my heart and my nerves, I slowly crawled back into bed, leaving the light on.

In the nightmare, Kenny and I were in the back seat of my parents' car as they were driving down the highway. Suddenly, they turn into Planet of the Apes parents with the ugly, ape-looking faces and hair all over their face and bodies, like wild animals. Then, they disappear into thin air, leaving the car without a driver or front-seat passenger. My brother and I look at each other and scream in fear, but quickly jump into the front seat. Almost instinctively, he grabs for the steering wheel, trying to avoid oncoming cars. Since I'm smaller, I go for the floorboard to maneuver the gas and brake, unsure of which is which. As we desperately trying to avoid a wreck, I wake up in a panic and sigh deeply, realizing it was only a dream.

I can remember, when I was young, hearing my parents argue, yell, and verbally fight. It didn't go on for long, and I don't remember it past age five. The uneasiness, stress, and tension that filled our home prior to my fifth birthday is still with me to this day. I remember the sick, helpless feeling I got as my mother and I jumped into the car and took off down the street, her mascara running down her face as she told me that she just needed a few minutes of quiet time to think and let things calm down. But, as a four-year-old child, you really think it's true—you really think that you and your mom are moving, without your dad and brother. This only happened once, and I recall vividly how I felt. This is the very reason I did not want a divorce. I did not want my kids to go through the feelings of insecurity and instability that I had felt in that moment. The reality, however, is that it happened to me and my children, and it happens to families around the world on a daily basis.

Unfortunately, what was only a nightmare for me is a reality that many children must face. It is important to remember that they are dealing with the trauma of a broken home with all of its emotional damage, scars, and collateral fallout.

Divorce-the Gift That Keeps on Giving

"I want a divorce!" For anyone who has heard those words or said those words to a spouse, there can be a wide range of emotions, a tidal wave of feelings that comes with those words.

Denial and anger are typically the first two stages of grief that people go through during loss, whether that loss is through death or divorce.

Grief.com gives a comprehensive view of the Five Stages of Grief, how to recognize what you are feeling, and how to navigate your way forward in your journey toward acceptance and wholeness. Starting with denial and anger, the grief process in a death is very similar to what most people experience during a divorce.

Going through a divorce is one of life's most stressful and painful times. I know; I've been there.

Divorce, whether you want it or not, makes you feel like you've been ran over by a Mack Truck and left for dead.

Marriage is the union of two people becoming one. It is no wonder that divorce hurts as much as it does—it is like we lose half of ourselves. Unfortunately, as much as divorce hurts grownups, the truth is that it's the children who suffer the most. Psychologists tell us that, the majority of the time, children of all ages internalize their parents' divorce in unhealthy ways and, often, they blame themselves.

Are You Ever Really PREPARED for Marriage?

Getting married is like having kids or going to war. No matter how much you prepare, you never really feel prepared—or, at least, I didn't.

I married young, I was 20, and my bride was 18. I graduated from my two-year college one weekend, my fiancée graduated high school the next weekend, and, the following weekend, we got married. Needless to say, it was a busy month. We had attended six weeks of marriage counseling, read a few of the prescribed books, and felt we were ready for a life of happiness and growing old together, raising kids. People have often asked why we married so young. I like to say, "We had to; we were in love." The fact is that people—especially people in the Midwest—married young. We got this from our parents and grandparents who grew up on the farm and married their neighbors. For those of us who wanted to wait to have sex until we were married, it often would cause couples to push the wedding date up, especially if you'd been dating for some time, like we had, three years! Fortunately, we had two years to get to know each other after we tied the knot before we had our first son. I think many couples miss out on this basic "get-to-know-each-other" phase by having kids right away.

I Made a Ton of Mistakes

Looking back, I was young, naïve, and very prideful and egotistical. I may have seemed to be a humble, coachable team player on the outside, but, on the inside I was compulsive, impatient and petulant.

Our First Fight

I remember our first fight happened the morning of our honeymoon. We were traveling, and I wanted a big breakfast, with eggs, biscuits, and all of the fixings, and my new wife just wanted a donut. I didn't have the skill set, nor wisdom and ability to communicate in a non-defensive manner, so that we could both get what we wanted. Instead, I got what I wanted, and we were both angry at each other for the rest of the day. The air between us was so cold, you could cut through the silence with a knife. This was not a good way to start a marriage. I was insecure, got offended when I felt my feelings weren't respected, and pushed love away, instead of creating an environment where it could flourish and grow.

For the next eight years, we had four sons: one every other year. In our first ten years of marriage, we did all of the things couples raising kids do: changing diapers, finding babysitters, reading books with our boy, rocking them to sleep, reciting nursery rhymes, going on family vacations, taking them to school, church, and sports, hosting play dates, teaching them how to read, walk, and talk, and, of course, trying to teach them not to kill their brothers.

CHAPTER 2

DON'T DIVORCE YOUR CHILDREN

It's easy to become self-absorbed and protective of our own feelings in divorce, because we are in so much pain that we forget about what our kids are going through. Depending on the age of your child, the best thing, in my own experience, is being present, asking questions, and listening to our kids and accepting their feelings, without judgment.

If they want to be angry, let them be angry. If they want to withdraw, let them withdraw. If they want to cuss you out, let them cuss you out. I don't think this is behavior they need to be punished for—they've just been through a divorce, too! I think it is a healthy way for them to express their hurt, anger, and grief, and for them to begin the healing process. If our children cannot feel safe to communicate their hurts to us in the midst of this very vulnerable time, who else will they be able to share them with?

I remember getting the call from the boys' mom when Josh was four. Josh had fallen off our front porch and the resulting knot on his head grew bigger than the size of Texas and faster than Pinocchio's nose. Of course, it freaked her out, and she wanted to take him to the emergency room. There was a nurse in our neighborhood who told us the real danger is if the knot does not come out; it is then that you have to be concerned with internal damage. I'd much rather see some ugly fits of anger, rage, and hurt from my kids now than ten or twenty years from now, if they are forced to internalize everything. Like the knot on my son's head, you need to let it come out, instead of letting it stay inside, causing internal damage of a different kind to them.

In chapter 7, How to Raise Emotionally Healthy Kids, I talk about a great resource called Divorce Recovery for kids *www.dc4k. org*, which is a great resource, and they typically have group sessions for the children at the same times/locations of Divorce Recovery for adults. *www.divorcecare.org* Having a safe place that kids can play, do activities, and talk with other kids and professional volunteers who specialize in divorce recovery is very valuable.

> ## I was in so much pain after my divorce that I was like the airline passenger in a crashing jet who FIRST needed to secure my own oxygen mask, before I helped my kids. I could eventually be there for my kids, but, first, I had to stabilize myself.

I borrowed this chapter title, *"Don't Divorce Your Children"*, from the book Don't Divorce Your Children by William A.H. Sammons, MD and Jennifer M. Lewis, MD, available on Amazon.

Doctors Sammons and Leis give some of the best advice you will find on the Internet ChildrenAndDivorce.com for keeping yourself and your kids sane through the divorce process.

Parent's Responsibilities in Divorce

During and after your divorce, there are certain responsibilities that you owe your children. Here are some of them:

1. Jointly tell the children about your decision to separate/ divorce.

2. Answer questions truthfully. Do not lie.

3. Do not substitute gifts for love and time and attention.

4. Facilitate visitation by the other parent at regular and predictable times.

5. Designate time for the children to spend individually with each parent.

6. Periodically discuss with your children their wishes about residence and visitation.

7. Actively participate in your children's lives.

8. Facilitate private communication with each parent by phone/mail/fax etc.

9. Encourage your children to understand the importance of maintaining both parental relationships.

10. Keep handover times free of inter-parental arguments and hostility.

11. Discuss your children's' feelings of guilt about causing the divorce.

12. Refrain from using your children as messengers between parents.

13. Refrain from using your children as hostages, or weapons against your ex-spouse.

14. Refrain from asking your children to keep secrets from the other parent.

15. Support relationships with both extended families.

16. Offer access to a neutral adult (therapist/teacher/ pediatrician/rabbi/priest) whose primary interest is the well-being of the children.

17. Help your children understand the terms of the divorce agreement, including financial, educational and visitation provisions.

18. Do not expose your children to your transient romantic relationships.

19. Do not abandon contact with your children under any circumstances.

The Rights Of Children

Drawing on our understanding of child development and our experience, we have constructed a list of children's rights, which are the cornerstone of our thinking. Recognizing these rights is the key to healthy and joyful post-divorce relationships with children.

- A lasting relationship with both parents
- Number one status in their parents' lives
- Parental cooperation throughout the divorce
- Truthful answers to their questions
- Relief from feelings of guilt and blame
- Freedom from inter-parental hostility
- Attention to their thoughts and feelings
- Input into the visitation schedule
- Privacy in communication with family and friends
- No displacement by competing relationships
- No requirement to parent their parents
- Freedom from the role of messenger
- No coercion to keep secrets
- An understanding of the divorce agreement

The above excerpt taken from the Website: childrenanddivorce.com

I think the main take away I want to give to you here in Chapter 2 is there are no right words or wrong words to say to your kids during a divorce. The main thing is: Be there for them, love them, ask them questions but don't pressure them to talk, they'll open up when they are ready and when they feel safe. Kids don't remember what we say, they remember how they feel when they are with us.

CHAPTER 3

MONEY STOP
THE BLEEDING

*"Marriage is grand, divorce
about a hundred grand."*

Anonymous

Few things can drain the bank like a divorce. Depending on which divorce/marriage expert or financial guru you talk to, you hear things like "A divorce will set you back seven years, etc." Like your boat capsizing in the middle of the Pacific
Ocean, a divorce can leave you feeling helpless, vulnerable, and susceptible to economic attack. Assuming finances have been a challenge for you, statistically, most divorces happen as a result of financial crisis. This section will help you take an honest inventory of where you are and how to improve your financial situation.

The first step you need to take in order to steady your finances as a divorcing single dad is:

1. Do an inventory.

Make a budget. On one side of a sheet of paper, write down all of the income and sources of revenue you have coming in each month, and, on the other side, write down every expense you can predict over the next 90, 180, and 365 days. Once you're done, add 20 percent to the expenses side, because there will be unexpected and unplanned surprises. From attorney's fees, to hiring babysitters, to moving fees, to additional work-related expenses, to going back to school to improve your hire ability and résumé, it is important to budget for the unforeseeable but almost certain extra expenses. Now, if you are fortunate enough to be in the black, good for you! Most newly divorced dads find themselves on the negative side of the balance sheet with this exercise.

> *"If your outgo exceeds your income - Your upkeep*
> *will be your downfall."*
> Tony Cooke

I heard recently on the radio that the average household debt in the U.S.— not including mortgage-related debt— has increased 20 percent a year. Families are spending more, but they are spending it on credit cards. While these numbers are good news for retailers in the short-term, the long-term financial impact for our families, our futures, and our nation as a whole is dismal. It is important to keep a close eye on finances throughout your divorce, or you may find yourself swimming in debt.

2. Downsize your overhead wherever you can.

This means eliminating all unnecessary and extra expenses, in order to survive financially. Talk with a good attorney and tax strategist or financial advisor to find out where it makes sense to cut expenses. Are you leasing a car? Perhaps, you are able to downgrade your car and drive an older model that is paid for, so you don't have a car payment for a few years. It could mean selling the house or leasing it out, in exchange for something smaller that does not require you to pour your money down an endless money pit and spend hours each month on maintenance. Remember, your kids will grow up and be gone before you know it. You can always reinvest in a big house or estate at a future date. Are you living on credit cards? Are you using credit cards to pay for groceries or utilities? Are you making only the minimum payments on credit cards? If yes, you are headed toward financial trouble, fast.

3. Become the Cash King – stop living on credit.

We live in a "buy now, pay later, I-want-it-all-now society". Few people have the discipline or patience to wait and pay for something only when they can afford it. But, believe it or not, that is the good old-fashioned way to getting rich. My parents retired at age 65 and don't have to work another day in their life, no matter how long they live. They've been able to do this because of the principles they lived by and taught me and my brother. Principles I have not always adhered to, but have always aspired to. If you can't afford it, don't buy it. Live a disciplined life, and don't spend money you really don't have. Credit cards are not cash, they are debts. They are shackles, a ball and chain that will keep you down. And, if you can't pay them off each month, they will slowly choke the financial air out of you, like a hungry python.

When I say become the cash king, that means pay cash for everything. Don't go in debt for anything, unless it is an income-producing vehicle, like a rental property or other investment.

Pay the credit cards off each month, so you don't rack up interest payments. Make the decision that the first month you can't pay the credit cards off, you will cut them up. Few have the discipline to do this, but, if you do, you are someone who can actually feel good about earning airline miles and other perks from credit card companies.

DaveRamsey.com is a valuable resource. His Financial Peace University has helped millions out of debt fast along with his helpful site EveryDollar.com.

4. Pick up an extra job to earn some extra cash.

Moonlighting—also called working a second job—is a great way for a cash-strapped dad or a dad who wants to build a financial reserve to hedge against future financial crisis to get ahead. Not only can a part time job provide extra income, it can become an outlet both socially and mentally to get a break from staring at the four walls of an empty, quiet, lonely apartment.

Growing up on a farm and seeing my dad's resourcefulness, I've always been able to produce cash very quickly and have never been out of work a single day of my life. I haven't always worked the jobs I've wanted, but I've always been able to pay my bills and keep the lights on. I've done many odd jobs and extra projects to earn money for myself and my family throughout the years, in addition to my regular career. There is a certain amount of sheer fear I faced as a dad when I learned babies three and four were on their way. But that momentary fear was replaced by the peace of knowing that I had all of resources in me to be a good provider and dad.

In addition to following my Seminary Bible School path of pastor, Christian educator, and youth minister, I've supplemented my income during lean times with: working retail, starting a janitorial company that grew to 12 full-time employees, Internet marketing, network marketing and direct sales, and, finally, my true passions of running a successful marketing firm and publishing company.

5. Adjust your W-2 withholdings.

If you are working a job and are a W-2 employee, you can increase your withholding allowances to put more money on your paycheck this week. I never wanted to give the government an interest-free loan. Some people like to get a few thousand back when they file their income tax return— not me; I always wanted my cash now. Ask an expert, but this can be a great way to increase weekly cash flow.

DISCLAIMER: I am not an attorney, a financial advisor, nor a CPA. You should check with qualified and competent advisors on all financial matters, but, after fifteen years of paying child support, four sets of braces, dental bills, doctor bills for too many broken bones and stitches to count, I've learned the importance of mastering your finances and planning for the future. Besides the usual expenses, over the years, there were the surprise expenses that would have crippled me, had I not been prepared, including: numerous surgeries on Jeremiah to attempt to repair a deaf ear, four rounds of chemo for Joshua, as well as a bone marrow transplant, appendectomy, and several other surgeries connected to his time in the hospital overcoming acute myloid leukemia. If you have kids, there will be emergencies, so plan accordingly.

6. Sell your junk.

That's right, have a good old-fashioned garage sale. You would be surprised how much you can make be selling your "junk". Many friends I suggest this to end up cashing in hundreds, even thousands of dollars, just by eliminating their junk.

7. Debt consolidation loan.

You can eliminate high-interest credit cards by getting a debt consolidation loan. This is good for managing high-interest-rate credit cards and only having one payment, instead of 16. The challenge with this is that many people will increase their spending and recharge their credit cards, landing them in more debt than before. If you can avoid making this mistake, it is a good option for you.

8. Emergency fund.

I subscribe to the Dave Ramsey philosophy of paying yourself first and having an emergency savings fund for accidents, incidents, and emergencies.

Are You a Disneyland Dad?

Sometimes, as a result of the guilt associated with a divorce and the guilt of not being there for the kids 24-7, some dads adopt a "Disneyland Dad" approach. While it's great to do fun things with your kids to help numb the pain of a divorce, over-compensating with this approach, especially if done to spite their mother or out of guilt for an affair, can be counterproductive.

Most kids just want quality chill time with dad; it doesn't have to be Disneyland every weekend.

Definition of **"Disneyland Dad"**, from the Urban Dictionary

Term used to describe the role that some divorced fathers fulfill, whereby they tend their biological children during certain prescribed times during the year (much like a vacation) rather than be a father full time.

Maria: You can take the children weekends during the summer.

Ted: No way! I'm not going to be a Disneyland Dad!

I remember after our divorce in 2001, just two months after 9/11, we were divorced. The boys were ten, eight, six, and four.

We had been separated since January; I was in my apartment and I wanted anything to go back to the way things were. I soon learned, however, that trips to the park, Chuck E. Cheese, the zoo, and church meant as much for my sons as Disneyland did at that point. This was a good thing, because, at the time, I could barely afford Chuck E. Cheese. Later, we went on to take some nice trips, but in the early days, I was pinching pennies anywhere I could. Many of those weekends involved extra espresso to keep up with my four sons.

They grow up so fast, but the time I was able to invest was worth it. Sure, when they got older, they didn't always want to come see me—they had their friends, their cars, and their jobs— so I valued the time I spent with them when they were little. Cherish the time you have with them, and have as much input as you can, for as long as you can. These are the relationships that really matter. The ones with your kids.

Extreme Housing Solution

When I was served divorce papers, it made sense for me to find an apartment. With four kids and working countless hours, it did not make sense for me to fight for custody and send the boys' mother out to work while I hired a nanny to take care of my sons, since their mom had been a stay-at-home mom for years. We agreed that she would stay in the house and deal with the day-to-day raising of the kids, and I would find an apartment and pay child support. This made the most sense for us, since I was only home to shower and sleep, anyway.

After a few years in the apartment, blowing money on rent, I really wanted to buy my own place to build up some equity again, but I wasn't in a place where I financially had 10 to 20 percent to put down on a house and get qualified for a traditional mortgage (this was before Fanny Mae and Freddy Mac made it easy for anyone to get into a home).

My solution: Buy a trailer, and move into into a mobile home park. In the back of my mind, I knew I could tell this trailer park story in the future to inspire someone. I was able to save $5,000 and went shopping for an RV. Since I just had the kids every other weekend, I figured it would be fun to "camp out" in the RV, and I'd be able to save some money, since I wasn't giving it to a landlord every month. I negotiated a good deal at one of the RV places I visited and bought a $9,000 RV for $5,000, cash and had it delivered to the mobile home park. It was 25 feet by 8 feet, a full 200 square feet—wow, my entire home was now smaller than the bedroom I grew up in on the farm as a kid! The next year, thanks to the money I saved, I was able to pay cash again, this time for a two-bedroom trailer with a complete laundry room, kitchen, and living room that doubled as my office. My youngest son, Jeremiah, now 18, still says his favorite house of mine was the one with wheels. His question: "Why didn't we ever take it anywhere?"

CHAPTER 4

DON'T BLAME THEIR MOM

It's easy to take sides in a divorce. It's easier to play the blame game than it is to take responsibility. Kids need a safe place to retreat to before, during, and after a divorce, and complaining about their mother and what she did or did not do will not help, but only hurt your child's emotional well-being.

Even if your kids' mom was the jerk in the relationship, it does not help your current situation to trash-talk her. Maybe she had an affair, was an unfit mom, lied, stole, cheated; none of that matters now. To dwell on the negativity in your past will only keep you, as the man, from moving forward, and it will stall your children's emotional health, as well.

One of the easiest things to do before, during, and after a divorce is to assign blame. It's easy to be the victim—it's hard to take responsibility. But, by taking responsibility, we are doing the best possible thing for our children. Children need to feel secure, loved, and protected. The best way for them to feel all of this is for us not to blame their mom for anything that has happened.

This does not mean we ignore the pain, but we choose not to burden our kids with this heavy burden. Instead, we choose to honor and show respect to their mother, and, by so doing, we foster a healthy feeling of security and trust in our children.

Not blaming their mother is one key factor in our sons and daughters feeling more secure and gives them a better shot at having successful relationships throughout life.

It's easy to say "don't blame their mom", but, when you have a few arrows—and, possibly, a few daggers in your heart—it may be very natural to want to slip back in to the "blame game", but doing so will only injure you more than you have been.

4 Positive Things that Happen For You When You Choose to Not Blame Their Mom

1. You feel better about yourself, because you start taking responsibility for what you need to take ownership of, like your feelings, your attitude, your actions, and your demeanor.

2. Since you feel better, your kids intuitively and immediately pick up on your new self-esteem boost, and they start feeling better about you and themselves.

3. Your kids are happier because you are happier.

4. Your kids feel better about you, which strengthens your relationship.

CHAPTER 5

DON'T GET STUCK IN YOUR MAN CAVE

I always wanted a man cave. You know that special room in the garage, basement, or attic where the wife and kids are not allowed (except on special occasions)? My dream man cave was furnished with a pool table, big-screen TV, leather recliner, and a sectional, so I could invite the guys over to watch games. It would even have a vintage soda machine and my favorite arcade games from the 80s: Pacman, Galaga, and Tron.

Even though I wanted the dream 'man cave', I never had one. Having four sons, practicality and budget won out over wish list desires every time. But, as guys, many times, we don't even need a physical man cave to retreat to. We retreat to our emotionally erected man caves of withdrawal, isolation, self-pity, addictions, or avoidance. The sad part is that many of us get stuck there for years.

Our emotional man caves become a prison of pain, fear, despair, and isolation. Because we withdraw, we never get the affirmation, emotional support, camaraderie, friendship, and intimacy we need to develop, grow, and mature, so we can be a positive blessing in our kids' lives and in our future spouses' life.

While having a safe place to retreat to is nice, especially if you have good, emotionally healthy guys who can help you walk through your pain and get you to the other side. Or a "virtual man cave" where you connect with guys who can help you on your journey of healing and recovery. But, when you are stuck in your man cave alone for days on end, excessively drinking, being sucked into the TV and avoiding things that need to be processed, confronted, healed, and dealt with, it can become unhealthy.

As guys, we are wired differently than our female counterparts— not just physically and mentally, but, also, emotionally. Face it: women like to be together, when they are happy or when they are down, heck, they even invite their friends to go to the bathroom with them. We, as guys, are not wired like that. Too much of the time, we suffer in silence and have a stoic, I-can-do-it-myself attitude. How many times have you told yourself, *I can make this work on my own or I've created this mess myself,* I will fix it all by myself. There is a place for independent thinking to get things done, but healing our kids is not the place for allowing our egos to get in the way of their peace and security.

Like the injured athlete who says, *"I've duct-taped my broken limbs up and taken some painkillers, Coach, can you put me back in the game?"* We get our fulfillment out of being the martyr, the hero, the rescuer, yet we are the one who needs to be saved, recued and healed, if we'd ever be brave enough to admit it to ourselves, much less anyone else. We are broken, and it's hard for us to admit it. It's hard to admit weakness, failure, or pain. But, by admitting our vulnerability, we can discover our greatest strength. In admitting our weakness and fears, we can find true strength, security, and peace. Imagine, just imagine, what that could do for our kids, when we find our true inner strength. Imagine how it could calm them down and bring them peace.

Do you have a mentor you meet with regularly to discuss your progress in the Divorce Recovery Cycle? On page 53 I give a complete list of resources to help single dad's not only survive but thrive.

5 Things Every Man Cave Needs

1. **Quite and solidarity**, so a dad can think, reflect, feel, question, ponder, ask questions, rest, forgive, and imagine and dream again.

2. **A notepad or legal pad and a pen**. Yes, a computer works, too, but I find that the old-fashioned legal pad and pen work best. There is something about writing down thoughts that engage your brain and willpower better than typing. Moreover, if you're on your computer, it is all-too-easy to get distracted with Facebook

3. **An hour each week to think, reflect, and pray.** It doesn't have to be in your cave, but can be, instead, in the car as you drive to work or as you take a walk or bike ride. Get into the habit of asking yourself: How am I feeling today? Why am I feeling this way? Is there anything I can do to change what I am feeling?

4. **An hour each week to phone a friend, mentor, or coach**. I had several guys who stood by my side during my divorce who were what I call "3 AM friends". 3 AM friends are the friends you can call at 3 AM when you need someone to talk to. Just knowing they were there gave me the emotional, mental, and spiritual strength and courage to know I'd come through the ordeal that was my divorce and that I'd be a better man for my kids on the other side. You need guys like this in your life.

5. **Start a new hobby, activity, or program**. As guys, we are doers, movers and action takers. Being divorced may leave you with many new hours in the week without your kids. Or, if your wife abandoned you, and you have zero free time, because all of your time away from work is filled with kids, make sure that you still find time for yourself. You will have to get creative to find time after the kids are in bed or before they wake up or on the weekends when they are at Grandma's. For me, it was running. I began training for my first marathon, which consumed a year of my life, but allowed me to meet some great new friends and achieve one of my lifelong bucket list goals.

CHAPTER 6

PARENTAL ALIENATION

This chapter was not in the first edition of this book, the e-book.
I've added it here, because the older I get, and the more guys I talk to, the more I see it: moms alienating dads and dads alienating moms.

Parental alienation (or hostile aggressive parenting) is a group of behaviors that are damaging to children's mental and emotional well-being, and can interfere with a relationship of a child and either parent. These behaviors most often accompany high-conflict marriages, separations, or divorces.

Find out more about parental alienation and hostile aggressive parenting at paawareness.org.

In the Bible, I Corinthians 13 is called "The Love Chapter". Although it can help us when we're married, it can help us even more when we're single.

I include it here from the NIV (New International Version):

4 Love is patient, love is kind. It does not envy, it does not boast, it is not proud. 5 It does not dishonor others, it is not self-seeking, it is not easily angered, it keeps no record of wrongs. 6 Love does not delight in evil but rejoices with the truth. 7 It always protects, always trusts, always hopes, always perseveres.

8 Love never fails. But where there are prophecies, they will cease; where there are tongues, they will be stilled; where there is knowledge, it will pass away. 9 For we know in part and we prophesy in part, 10 but when

completeness comes, what is in part disappears. 11 When I was a child, I talked like a child, I thought like a child, I reasoned like a child. When I became a man, I put the ways of childhood behind me. 12 For now we see only a reflection as in a mirror; then we shall see face to face. Now I know in part; then I shall know fully, even as I am fully known.

13 And now these three remain: faith, hope and love. But the greatest of these is love.

It's important our kids feel love in our home. They need to feel genuine love not just performance based love of: "Daddy will love you if you are good." We need to love them unconditionally, just like God loves us. I'm not talking about behavior modification and discipline here. I'm talking about if we don't have a base-line of love, trust and security our kids won't act right regardless. When children feel secure, at peace, nurtured and loved they will get the emotional and spiritual foundation they need to thrive in life.

CHAPTER 7

FACING YOUR FEAR

"If you live in fear of the future because of what happened in your past, you'll end up losing what you have in the present."

SingleDadsThrive.com

Nothing paralyzes more than fear, and nothing is more freeing than facing your fear and overcoming your fear. Fear of the unknown is what gripped me most after my divorce.

Questions bombarded my mind 24-7 with their relentless assault:

- Was I worthless as a father as a dad and as a husband?
- If I were a good man, why did my ex-wife want a divorce?
- Will I marry again? Will I love again?
- Will I be alone the rest of my life?
- Will I always feel like people are staring at me when I walk into a room?

When it comes to overcoming fear, many times, the real issue is control. As men, we have the need to feel in-control, and a divorce throws our life into a tailspin, a downward spiral that makes us feel out-of-control, anxious, and at a loss to know what to do. We may find ourselves depressed, worried, anxious, turning to addictive behavior—like drinking or sex, being avoidant, missing work, or having other problems. We may be so deep in thought and depression that we wreck our car or arrive at a destination and wonder how we got there, since we don't remember driving there.

When you deal with the anxiety, you can minimize the paralyzing affects of fear.

Here are a few tips that I find helpful in neutralizing my fears and anxieties after my divorce:

1. **Utilize deep breathing techniques to calm yourself.**

   To take a calming, deep breath, start by inhaling fully, then holding it, and, finally, slowly exhaling. Take ten really deep breaths. Getting more oxygen to your brain and blood will help calm your nerves.

2. **Talk to a licensed counselor, therapist, or pastor.**

   By talking to a professional that is trained in divorce recovery, you can deal proactively with fear, anger, and the other emotions of self-sabotage that often come with a debilitating divorce. Counselors and trained professionals are equipped to help you navigate your way successfully through this time in your life. Going to a counselor is not an admission of guilt; it is a sign of strength and wisdom on your part. Don't suffer in silence – reach out for help.

   Just like taking your car in for maintenance, sometimes, we dads just need a tune up, but, after a divorce, we need an overhaul. Once we are "back on the road", routine maintenance and oil changes are important to check in and talk about how we are doing.

3. **Recognize the spiritual dimension of your life.**

   Recently, I was talking with a divorced dad who is 49 years old. He had been very successful in his business, but his divorce had hurt him very deeply, and his kids are with their mom, living in a different country. He said, "You know, I only recently discovered the spiritual aspect to my life. To think I missed out on this for so many years." By getting in touch with our spiritual needs as men we can allow God to do a deep work in us that is not merely surface or cosmetic, after all the heart transformation can and will make a difference as we live out our lives on this planet and others will notice.

By doing a spiritual inventory and meeting with your Pastor, Priest or Rabbi a Single Dad can begin or restart the journey toward spiritual wholeness.

CHAPTER 8

OVERCOMING ANGER

While I struggled with many aspects of my divorce, one of the biggest hurdles for me to overcome was facing and dealing with my anger. On the therapist's sofa a year after my divorce, I broke down and cried—I admitted to my counselor that I did not feel the pain until a full year after the divorce. I had hardened my heart so much to try and build up immunity to the pain, but, by not allowing myself to feel for years, what I created, instead, was a raging inferno of anger.

Fourteen years after my divorce, this is still tough for me to write about. I look back on the façade I had created: the picture-perfect image of a happy marriage, smiling on the outside, while all the while dying and hurting on the inside, feeling all alone and not knowing who to talk to.

From everyone else's point of view, we had a happy marriage, a good marriage. It wasn't until ten years into the marriage that my anger began to seethe to the top like hot lava erupting from an exploding volcano. What was going on? This wasn't me. Why did little things set me off? It just did not make sense. I didn't understand what was happening, and it would be years before I truly understood what was going on. Even after hundreds of hours and thousands of dollars on the therapy couch and in group therapy did I begin to realize the truth: I had ignored my needs, emotions, and feelings as a man for years, which created a growing ocean of bitterness, resentment, and Most of all, I had created self-hatred, because, deep down, I knew that I was not being true to who I was. As a result of not being true to myself, there was no way that I could love my family the way God designed me to love them, nor could I receive his love for me, because I had an underlying self-hatred going on that I could not even conceptualize, much less verbalize or understand.

All I knew when we divorced was that I had developed an anger problem, but, for the life of me, I could not figure out why. I had never been a particularly angry person. I had a good childhood and exceptional upbringing. There was no apparent reason why I should be so angry. I asked myself; "are men just wired this way? Is this normal?" One minute, I would be enjoying life, and, then, someone could say something wrong or look at me the wrong way, and BAM!, I'd explode like an atomic bomb. Then, embarrassed, I would apologize to everyone and go for a walk and try to calm down.

4 Steps to Get Control Over Anger

1. **Anger always has an underlying issue.**

   From fear, to insecurity, to financial stress, to feeling disrespected, there is always something causing the anger, even if it isn't immediately apparent. Look at what is driving the anger, and deal with the root cause. If you are not able to identify the cause, you may want to seek the guidance of a therapist or life coach, so that you are able to deal with the problem at its root and move on with your life as an emotionally healthy individual.

2. **Don't ignore it – address it.**

   While it is easy to bury your head in the sand, ignoring a problem does not make it go away. The only way to make a problem go away is to face it head-on and find a solution.

   By ignoring a problem, like your mounting credit card debt, it only makes the problem worse. If you determine that financial stress and fear are driving your anger, ask yourself, How can I improve my financial situation and minimize my stress? Whatever is causing your anger, ask yourself the tough questions that will prompt you to find a solution and start reducing your anger.

3. **Find a group of guys who have overcome anger.**

   Learn from them how they overcame. Hear their stories share your story with them. This is where I again recommend visiting a CelbrateRecovery.com group in your area or a DivorceCare.org group, both have awesome anger recovery programs that can not only address the symptom of anger but get to the root cause and help you detonate that ticking time bomb on the inside of you.

4. Walk away from volatile situations.

Once you identify the people or the person who angers you, you can avoid them. Always ask yourself WHY? For example, when you ask yourself, "Why does this person anger me"? You are able to really examine your feelings and get to the root of your anger. While you are learning how to manage your anger better, it is important that you do not put yourself into a situation where you know you will likely explode. It's not being cowardly; It's being smart.

CHAPTER 9

HOW TO RAISE EMOTIONALLY HEALTHY CHILDREN

If a divorce rocks your world, consider that it rocks your kids' worlds ten times more. Kids of every age need both parents, when possible. Unless your ex is a drug addict, or is emotionally, verbally, or mentally abusive, chances are that they will benefit from spending time with both of you.

Here are a few things that worked for me, when I was trying to raise emotionally healthy children in the midst of a divorce that was tearing their worlds apart:

1. **Build a support network of friends and family to help with the kids.**

    From grandparents, to church members, to neighborhood friends, to babysitters, to nannies, you should have a stable of paid and unpaid caregivers, so, when you find yourself in an emergency, you will always have backups to help you out when Grandma is in Boca or the babysitter is cramming for finals.

2. **Make sure your kids have someone to talk to.**

    Just like you can't internalize everything that you are feeling, your kids need a safe place to vent, question, and process the divorce and how it's affecting them. Don't expect them to open up all at once. Give them time and space to open up to you when they are ready. It's enough to let them know that they can talk to you if and when they want.

3. **Make sure your kids know that the divorce is not their fault.**

Psychologists tell us that most kids blame themselves for their parents' divorce. Tell them it is not their fault. You will need to reassure them of this for many years.

The affect of divorce on kids

http://en.wikipedia.org/wiki/Holmes_and_Rahe_stress_scale

Remember the Holmes and Rahe Stress Scale I introduced on page 8? They've created the same scale for kids and it's pretty mind blowing. A modified scale has also been developed for non-adults. Similar to the adult scale, stress points for life events in the past year are added and compared to the rough estimate of how stress affects health.

...for non adults

Event	Mean value	Event	Mean value
Death of parent	100	Jail sentence of parent for over 30 days	53
Unplanned pregnancy/abortion	100	Breaking up with boyfriend or girlfriend	53
Getting married	95	Beginning to date	51
Divorce of parents	90	Suspension from school	50
Acquiring a visible deformity	80	Becoming involved with drugs or alcohol	50
Fathering a child	70	Birth of a brother or sister	50
Jail sentence of parent for over one year	70	Increase in arguments between parents	47
Marital separation of parents	69	Loss of job by parent	46
Death of a brother or sister	68	Outstanding personal achievement	46
Change in acceptance by peers	67	Change in parent's financial status	45
Unplanned pregnancy of sister	64	Accepted at college of choice	43
Discovery of being an adopted child	63	Being a senior in high school	42
Marriage of parent to stepparent	63	Hospitalization of a sibling	41
Death of a close friend	63	Increased absence of parent from home	38
Having a visible congenital deformity	62	Brother or sister leaving home	37
Serious illness requiring hospitalization	58	Addition of third adult to family	34
Failure of a grade in school	56	Becoming a full fledged member of a church	31
Not making an extracurricular activity	55	Decrease in arguments between parents	27
Hospitalization of a parent	55	Decrease in arguments with parents	26
		Mother or father beginning work	26

Score of 300+: At risk of illness.
Score of 150-299: Risk of illness is moderate. (reduced by 30% from the above risk)
Score <150: Slight risk of illness.

CHAPTER 10

OVERCOMING CANCER, OVERCOMING ANYTHING

I was flying to speak in North Carolina when I got the call from the boy's mom. "The Doctors say Josh has the most aggressive form of leukemia, and they are doing surgery and starting chemotherapy tomorrow," she stated. Nothing prepares you for a moment like this.

I had been with Josh the day before. We had prayed for him, because he had been complaining of pain. His mother suspected that he may be suffering from "growing pains"; all we knew for certain was that our son was suffering and that the ibuprofen wasn't enough to stop the pain. My ex-wife told me that she would take Josh to a checkup the next day. Thinking that it was all routine, I was completely stunned by the call.

And that was only the beginning. Six months later, Josh was looking at four rounds of chemo, a bone marrow transplant, an appendectomy, and other surgeries. Fortunately, his faith in God's healing power was unwavering, and his two oldest brothers were perfect bone marrow matches. I was so proud of my sons; they even fought over who'd get the chance to save Josh's' life. Michael won in the end, because Matt had a slight cold the week of the transplant. Witnessing my son's supernatural faith in God and the miracles that accompanied

this time in the hospital showed me God's Grace at work in life during a time of divorce. This difficult time for our family required me to rely on God's Grace, faithfulness, and goodness to bring me peace, hope, and healing.

When Josh's' mom told me that he would be starting chemotherapy the next day, my first reaction was to suggest that we get a second opinion and talk to a naturopathic doctor at Cancer Treatment Centers of America. After phoning my attorney and calling the court in Oklahoma, I quickly learned that, as the non-custodial parent, I had no right or say in my son's treatment. As it turned out, she made the right decision in the situation as the custodial parent, and I'm glad God gave her and Josh the grace and wisdom to know the best plan of action at the time.

Although the situation turned out in the end, realizing that I was completely powerless over my son's treatment emphasized to me that, as a divorcing parent, it is of paramount importance that you talk to your attorney about your rights as a single dad and get the correct words into your divorce decree if you want to have a legal say in your children's medical care. Be incredibly careful about how your divorce decree is worded. Depending on what state you live in and what your divorce decree say's you may or may not have any say in the medical treatment of your child. Fortunately for Josh and our family, the treatment worked, and Josh is cancer-free.

CHAPTER 11

MOVING ON

Life is all about movement. If we're not moving forward, we are dying. If we are not growing, maturing, learning , and exploring, we are atrophying, diminishing, and shrinking. When I say "moving on", I'm not talking about moving on from your kids. I'm talking about moving on away from your hurt, pain, damage, emotional scars, and the collateral damage of your divorce that left indelible scars on your soul. Moving forward, embracing the good, and leaving the bad, with all of its residual pain. If you are in the throes of pain now, you might be thinking, Do I even want to live? Will I love again? Will I feel whole again? The answer to all of these questions is yes. Although it may not feel like it right now, there will come a time when you will feel whole again and be ready to love again and live your life to the fullest.

What is Recovery Time, and Why Do I Need It?

Recovery time is necessary to heal from past pain, wounds and trauma. Just like resting between workouts at the gym, the soul and the spirit need recovery time before starting another intimate relationship involving dating, intimacy, and soul-to-soul connection. Most experts agree that some recovery time and protocols are recommended to ensure future relational success, before starting another intimate relationship.

At this point, many a man will say, Maybe for other guys, but I am the exception. I don't need recovery time. These are the men who fall the hardest. Relationships with the opposite sex are more powerful than any drug. They not only give us endorphin releases, but also stroke our male ego, providing us with feeling accepted, a higher self-esteem, and satisfying our need to be needed and our need for sexual fulfillment. This "drug" can hurt us more quickly and deeply in the fresh wound of a divorce, if we are not wise to how this works on our psyche and our soul when our wounds are still fresh.

Besides, why would we want to bring a woman to fall in love with us, when we are not yet emotionally healed from our past relationship? It's easy to hide our shortcomings, our hang-ups, and our issues when dating, but don't be fooled and believe the lie many men tell themselves. Hiding our issues is not the same as overcoming our issues. We all need some recovery time and some therapy time, before we start down the road of another intimate relationship.

When it comes to divorce recovery, DivorceCare.org recommends one year of recovery for every four years of marriage. Now, before you flush this stat down the toilet, check out their Website and read more at   DivorceCare.org

CHAPTER 12

DATING AGAIN

Humans desire relationships. We are built to crave intimacy. The challenge with dating too soon after a divorce is that if we don't first deal with our pain, trauma, and emotional baggage of the previous relationship, we will, without question, carry our hurts, habits, and hang-ups into the next relationship.

How much time for recovery?

Pain is a good thing. It let's us know there is a problem and something is not right. As dads, we should not see to fix the symptom of pain, but the reason for the pain. In so doing, we can, ultimately, have what we want: love, respect, understanding, and intimacy.

Pain is a signal to alert us that SOMETHING IS WRONG.

Six months before turning 40, I realized that I wanted to run a marathon before my 40th birthday. The normal time one should train for a marathon is a year, but, being the overconfident and impatient guy that I was, I jumped in and started training. One thing that I did right in training for the marathon was that I joined a running group, and several times a week—including Saturday—we would get together at 5 AM to run and train. What I did wrong was that I did not give my body enough time to prepare for a marathon.

When my friends were running the half marathon, I had to set it out and cheer them on from the sidelines, because I was suffering with shin splints. Like newly divorced dads, many new runners underestimate the amount of recovery time that is necessary to be healthy, whole, and optimally prepared to not only enjoy, but also to maintain a new relationship.

My goal was to run a "sub-five" marathon, my first marathon in less than five hours. Well, I ran it in five hours and five minutes.

The toughest part for me was thinking that I was at mile 18 and being disappointed when I saw that I was only at mile marker 16!

At the end of the race though, my four sons jumped up from the spectator viewing area and ran the last three miles of the race with me. That memory is one of the major highlights of my life. I've replayed the scene of the five of us crossing the finish line together many times in my head. It meant so much to me that we were together, and and that they wanted to be with me while I finished the journey that I had trained for. It was symbolic of our journey as five men on the road of life together.

We owe it to ourselves, our future partner, and our kids to fix what is broken in ourselves, before dragging them and a new spouse into a new relationship, all the while opening old wounds from the past. We looked at reasonable recovery times in the previous chapter, so I won't go in too deeply again here. The main thing to realize is that "recovery time" is never wasted time. Every athlete has to take days off after training or competing in their sport, no matter how grueling or docile their sport is. The body, mind, and spirit need to recalibrate, and that is just the way we are built. We can try to rush God's healing process, but, if we do, we are likely to re-damage an old injury and be worse off than we were before.

CHAPTER 13

GIVING BACK – 30STORIES, 30 MEN, 30 DAYS

I felt compelled to share 30 stories, from 30 men, for 30 days, leading up to Father's Day 2016. It seemed easy enough, because, all around us, there are dads who are making a difference, who are quietly just going about their lives, without fanfare.

As I found it, it was a challenge to collect the stories, and here is why:

1. **Single dads are busy.**

   Single dads are extremely busy. Dads who are really making a difference are not looking for a microphone or a soapbox they just want to leave the world a better place for their kids – and I get that.

2. **Men don't get the props they deserve.**

   In our modern culture, men have been marginalized. What do I mean by this? I mean that, for the past 40 years, culture has tried to minimize men, in order to lift up women. The
   reality is you don't have to put down one sex to elevate the other. True men of character have humbly avoided the limelight, the applause, and the affirmation, but I think that as a society, we have suffered from this influence. Because we have not fully honored our good men, our young children have suffered.

   Media and pop culture glamorize and deify athletes, celebrities, and artists who make millions but are abusive, compulsive, and destructive. I want to see the truly good men and good dads who are showing up for their kids, respecting the women in their lives, paying child support, instilling spiritual values, and leaving a lasting legacy for their kids get some well-deserved honor and airtime.

I'm in search of these men. I want them to tell the world their stories.

3. **Men need a platform.**
They need a platform, a voice, and a megaphone, to inspire future generations and make their kids stronger, healthier, more secure, and happy.

CHAPTER 14

The Art of Letting Go

One of the hardest things for us to do as men because we are wired by God to be achievers, providers and protectors is to let go. Once we realize that a divorce is inevitable it's hard to actually let go emotionally. If we don't have custody of our kids or if we have joint custody it can be very unnerving when our daily routine is changed due to a divorce, child custody or court ordered decrees and mandates.

The first key in moving forward and maintaining our sanity is to emotionally learn how to let go. It's good for us and it's good for our kids' emotional well-being as well.

The best way to let go and move on is to learn to accept what we cannot change. Accepting what we cannot change takes humility and gratitude but is the quickest path toward healing for us and our kids.

"God, grant me the serenity to accept the things I cannot change, Courage to change the things I can, and wisdom to know the difference." Reinhold Niebuhr

CONCLUSION

The principles, tips, and ideas I've presented in this book are to help you reconnect with your kids and to help you and them move on with your lives as successfully as possible after a divorce. We all have different goals and different objectives, but, if your goal is to be an emotionally healthy parent who has emotionally healthy kids who love and respect you and have healed and gained enough self-awareness to have healthy and meaningful relationships, we've achieved our goal.

I really believe the root issue with everything in life is spiritual. I believe we are all spiritual beings on this planet and we cannot truly love and be loved until we find the author of salvation our
Creator, Jesus Christ. Below, I include the 12 Steps of Celebrate Recovery that have helped me and many thousands of others over the years to reconnect with our spiritual roots and overcome the hurts, habits, and hang-ups that keep us trapped in a cycle of defeat.

Celebrate Recovery 12 Steps

CelebrateRecovery.com

1. We admitted we were powerless over our addictions and compulsive behaviors, that our lives had become unmanageable.
2. We came to believe that a power greater than ourselves could restore us to sanity.
3. We made a decision to turn our wills and our lives over to the care of God.
4. We made a searching and fearless moral inventory of ourselves.

5. We admitted to God, to ourselves, and to another human being the exact nature of our wrongs.

6. We were entirely ready to have God remove all these defects of character.

7. We humbly asked Him to remove all our shortcomings.

8. We made a list of all persons we had harmed and became willing to make amends to them all.

9. We made direct amends to such people whenever possible, except when to do so would injure them or others.

10. We continued to take personal inventory and when we were wrong, promptly admitted it.

11. We sought through prayer and meditation to improve our conscious contact with God, praying only for knowledge of His will for us and power to carry that out.

12. Having had a spiritual experience as the result of these steps, we tried to carry this message to others and to practice these principles in all our affairs.

Things You Can do With Kids (Other than TV):

Cooking

Free classes at your local Boys and Girls Club, YMCA, YWCA, Church, Library or Community Event Center

Shopping

Reading

Field Trips:
- Zoo-by using season passes, you can easily save money.
- Museums.
- Hobby Lobby, Michael's Crafts, Home Depot and Lowes – Has weekend workshops for kids on a number of projects and topics in the "DIY" "How-To" category.

Find single parent resource and groups in your area by looking online, on Facebook.com/events, and on Meetup.com

GLOSSARY OF TERMS

Selfie: You will want to take lots of these, especially when your kids are young.

Selfie Stick: a stick for taking pictures with you and your kids with your smartphone, so you don't need a photographer. They normally sell for $15 or less online.

Disneyland Dad: A dad who tries to make up for poor parenting and divorce by outdoing and out-spending Mom to try and buy love from his children.

Debt Consolidation Loan: A loan to consolidate your debts.

Words of Affirmation: One of the five love languages for kids and something you will want to give them daily.

Emergency Fund: The fund you keep in a savings account and have three to six months worth of income saved, in case you get laid off work or have an accident.

RESOURCES:

Money

Dave Ramsey DaveRamsey.com
EveryDollar.com
Credit Repair CreditKarma.com
Clark Howard ClarkHoward.com

Divorce Care

DivorceCare.org
Divorce Care for Kids dc4k.org

divorcesource.com divorcenet.com childrenanddivorce.com
Overcoming Anger apa.org/topics/anger/control.aspx

Dealing with Grief and Loss
Grief.com

ADDITIONAL RESOURCES

Book the 5 Love Languages for Kids 5LoveLanguages.com
SingleDadsThrive.com
FreeAdvice.com
FocusontheFamily.com

No one group has had more of an impact on me personally as a man in my
post-divorce recovery than these three friends I'm about to introduce you to.
They have sold millions of books, are New York Times Best-Selling Authors,
have helped thousands of men and you will see why when you go to their
Website or read one of their many books.

DR. STEPHEN ARTERBURN

NewLife.com

Author of the Every Man's Battle Series on Sexual Integrity, Healing is a Choice, Regret-Free Living, Lose it for Life and many more

DR. HENRY CLOUD

DrCloud.com

Too many books to mention but most famous for his breakthrough book on Boundaries with Dr. John Townsend, Boundaries: When to Say Yes, How to Say No to Take Control of Your Life, Necessary Endings and How To Get A Date Worth Keeping: Be Dating In Six Months Or Your Money Back

DR. JOHN TOWNSEND

DrTownsend.com

Some of his books in addition to the boundary series with Dr. Henry Cloud are: Safe People, Who's Pushing Your Buttons, The Mom Factor, Hiding from Love, Boundaries for Kids, etc....

Also deserving of a look is:

Author, Speaker, Coach

JOHN ELDRIDGE

Author of the Wildly popular "Wild at Heart Series for Men"

RansomedHeart.com

ABOUT THE AUTHOR

Michael D. Butler found himself a single dad of four sons, ages ten, eight, six, and four in 2001. Now, his sons are 26, 24, 22, and 20, carving out their own space in life and writing their own stories—he is very proud of them.

Michael's first career after Bible School was Pastoral
Ministry, which was a good transition into his second career: entrepreneurship. Being an entrepreneur gave him the financial and time freedom to maximize his time with his sons when they were young.

As a marathoner, one of the proudest moments of Michael's life was when his four sons ran the last three miles of the Route 66 Marathon in Tulsa, Oklahoma with him in 2008 at ages 18, 16, 14 and 12. After his divorce was final in 2002, he found DivorceCare.org, which offered a huge support and resource to Michael, who later began assisting as a group facilitator. Now, he runs a growing movement of men at SingleDadsThrive.com, where he, along with other men, encourage their divorced dad friends to not only survive, but thrive after a divorce and share stories and resources to do just that. **Check out 30 Stories 30 Dads 30 Days** on SingleDadsThrive.com perhaps you will see someone you know? His "Day Job" is running   BeyondPublishing.net helping Authors get their books and brand to the world.

NOTES

NOTES

NOTES

NOTES

NOTES

NOTES

NOTES

NOTES

NOTES

NOTES

NOTES

NOTES

NOTES

NOTES

NOTES

NOTES

CPSIA information can be obtained
at www.ICGtesting.com
Printed in the USA
FSOW04n2343290817
37985FS